A SINGLE MOTHER'S GUIDE TO RAISING A SON

A SINGLE MOTHER'S GUIDE TO RAISING A SON

Mervin A. Bourne Jr.

Copyright 2016 Mervin A. Bourne Jr.

All rights reserved. No part of this book may be reproduced in any form, stored in a retrieval system, or transmitted in any form or by any means—electronic, mechanical, digital, photocopy, recording, or other—without permission in writing from Mervin A. Bourne Jr. except in the case of brief quotations embodied in critical articles or reviews.
First Edition
Cover design by:
Michael Tudor Jr., www.paperface.carbonmade.com
Internal artwork by:
Michael Tudor Jr., www.paperface.carbonmade.com and
Elijah Bourne
Poetry contributed by Chloe Bourne

ISBN-13: 9780997689600
ISBN-10: 0997689609

I hope you enjoy this book. It is meant to empower, enlighten, and encourage. If you are a single mother raising a boy, by choice or not, or you know a single mother raising a boy, thank you for reading, gifting, or sharing this book. The love, pain, and wisdom of thousands of lives went into its making.
Thank you.
www.mervinbourne.com

*To Elijah and Chloe, the reason for everything I do.
Be better than me. Be the best you possible.
Seek your purpose, then live it.*

CONTENTS

Introduction: You Are Not Alone, and This Book Is for *You* · · · · · · · · · · · · · · xi

Part I	Loving, Spoiling, and Creating the Entitlement Monster · · · · · · · · · · · · · · · ·	1
Chapter 1	Are You Creating a Monster? · · · · · · · · · · ·	3
Chapter 2	The Difference between Loving and Spoiling ·	8
Chapter 3	The Real World and Respecting the Theory of Consequence · · · · · · · · · · · · ·	14
Chapter 4	Running from Resentment into the Arms of Regret · · · · · · · · · · · · · · · · · ·	22
Part II	Are You Destroying Your Son's Self-Worth? ·	25
Chapter 1	Which Side Are You On? · · · · · · · · · · · ·	27
Chapter 2	Hiding Is a Habit, but So Is Achieving · · ·	36
Chapter 3	Creating Opportunities for Greatness · · ·	43
Chapter 4	The Measure of Worth: Are You Sending a Clear Message? · · · · · · · · · · · ·	48

Part III	Raising a Goal-Oriented Son Begins with You (Not Your Son) · · · · · · · · · · · · 53
Chapter 1	Seeing, Thinking, and Living Beyond Today · 55
Chapter 2	Building a Foundation for a Goal-Setting Son · · · · · · · · · · · · · · · · · 58
Chapter 3	The Short Sell · 64
Chapter 4	The Goal-Setting Boy Becomes the Goal-Setting Man · · · · · · · · · · · · · · · · 70
Chapter 5	High School, College, and the Real World · 73
Chapter 6	Wanting It and Getting It: The Great Divide · · · · · · · · · · · · · · · · · · · 77
Part IV	The Necessity and Power of Mentoring: Where Do I Begin? · · · · · · · · · · · · · · · · 79
Chapter 1	The Value of Mentoring · · · · · · · · · · · · · 81
Chapter 2	Where and How to Find Mentors · · · · · · · 84
Chapter 3	Mentoring and Defining Manhood · · · · · 88
	Epilogue: Dare · 93

INTRODUCTION

YOU ARE NOT ALONE, AND THIS BOOK IS FOR *YOU*

FROM THE AGE of eleven, I was raised by a single mother. Before writing this book, I asked God to give me the wisdom, confidence, and clarity of mind to convey how my life experiences and observations could help millions of single mothers struggling with and agonizing over the daunting task of successfully raising a young boy to be a man. I put emphasis on *successfully* because millions of single mothers are raising boys to the age of eighteen (and beyond) and will be doing so for years to come. But we don't need experts to tell us that despite some of their best efforts, something is going terribly wrong on a mass scale.

Everyone has his or her own definition of success. To some, it means attaining a certain income; to others, it means driving a certain car. To still others, it means gaining fame and notoriety, while for some, it means graduating from high school or college. In my eyes, however, being successful means that you have identified your talents and gifts and are using them as a means to fulfill your obligations to yourself, your family, and your fellow man. If money, fame, and notoriety come with the fulfillment of those obligations, then so be it. I truly believe that if boys are raised to believe that their happiness and success depends on whether or not they identify and develop their talents and strengths for the fulfillment and betterment of themselves and the people around them, then the world would be a much different place. Families would be tighter and stronger, and our boys and men would be more responsible; they would be "successful" in mass proportions.

Unfortunately, most fathers are not in the home with their children. Many full-time parents, most of whom are single mothers, are not teaching these concepts, or, when they try to, their sons are not buying into these concepts. It is apparent that our boys have instead bought into a destructive ideology of resource-driven self-definition—that is, believing that their worth and value are defined by and limited to their material resources. This ideology is destructive for many reasons, including the fact that it denies them the empowerment synonymous with knowing that they are inherently valuable. Moreover, this resource-driven ideology causes them to see the people around them and society as nothing more than the resources for their needs, wants, and desires. They also grow up to be men who believe that their presence on earth serves no purpose other than daily survival, accented by sporadic moments of pleasure in a world that has made no way for them.

Understandably, single mothers are up against many opposing outside forces and influences that are making their daily mission seem impossible. The result has been an entire subclass of society that does not believe that they are obligated to do better than they are doing. They have recognized many of the obstacles that lie before them, but have not been taught to recognize, confront, and overcome the obstacles that lie within them.

Our sons do not believe that the key to their lack of fulfillment, their mediocrity, and their unhappiness lies within them. Our sons are not buying into the truth that nothing external can define them or limit them without permission—not their clothes, their shoes, their tattoos, the number of children they father, their cars, their sexual relationships, their platonic relationships, or what the world thinks of them. These sons—once boys—become men whose sense of self is inextricably tied to material possessions they have, desire, or are willing to die trying to obtain. These boys become men who are infinitely unfulfilled because they have been taught that their worth is tied up and inextricably intertwined with external validation, material possessions, and the number of women they reproduce with, rather than the spirit of the universal God within them.

In numbers large enough to be shameful, our young men are not graduating from high school, going to college, or acquiring trades that will enable them to support themselves or the families they prematurely create.

They are not dreaming, and if they were ever bold enough to have dreams, they are not doing what it takes to fulfill them or live them. Our sons are finding themselves entangled with the criminal justice system and otherwise totally unprepared to face the harsh realities of life. They are chronically underachieving, blaming the world (and their mothers) for their failures and shortcomings. They are afraid to try and afraid to fail. Often behind very brave and macho exteriors, they are boys who lack the fundamentals to excel independently at anything in life.

Young men being raised by single mothers have turned into an entire subclass of people who find their dreams—if they have any at all—deferred. They struggle with the reality that the world offers no sympathy for their underachievement and no free passes because they grew up in a single-parent household without all of the physical, emotional, intellectual, and financial benefits that come with having a responsible, loving father in the home. It does not, however, logically follow that boys raised in two-parent homes are automatically winners of the success lottery and immune to all the pitfalls that ensnare other boys. Nothing could be further from the truth. The main idea of this book is not "if he had a father in the house everything would be perfect."

However, one theme that does pervade this book is that pretending the single-parent and two-parent dynamics are the same—for the sake of political correctness—is both selfish and self-destructive. Similarly, pretending that a mother's financial success and independence insulates her and her son from the realities of the endeavor that is raising a boy as the primary (or sole) caretaker is also a politically correct ideology not espoused in this book. To this point, most mothers, mothers-to-be, guardians, and mentors (anyone actively influencing the life of another) who have been introduced to the premise of this book have responded with some form of "thank you—what took you so long?" However, plenty have conversely responded either in anger—or with at least the side eye—at the concept of tackling this issue from any perspective other than an attack on absent, neglectful fathers who don't pay child support.

What I have found myself explaining (with a high degree of success), is that this book is not meant to be merely a collection of philosophical musings or intellectual rants that serve no purpose other than self-adulation, or an extended pat on the back for already-extraordinary mothers. There are plenty of other books on the market for those purposes, and they have their (very popular and profitable) lane. This book, however, is meant to be an immediate (not future), practical (not ideological), honest (not sugarcoated), humble (not accusatory), loving (not politically correct) body of information to help any woman raising a boy without a man in the home—right now. I'm talking about the woman who has boys asleep in the next room right now; the woman who will wake up tomorrow morning, feed hungry mouths, and send them to school; the woman whose twelve-year-old son now looks at her eye to eye when he stands up; the woman whose fifteen-year-old son towers over her and is no longer afraid of her small hand or her mouth; the woman who has "a good job" and plenty of money in the bank, but whose son still yearns to figure out the man within him (the one connected to *his purpose*—not his possessions or his girlfriends) that his mommy can never decipher *for* him or demonstrate to him; the woman who has it all figured out but knows deep down inside that the best tool in her belt is the perception of her strength or her ability to give her son whatever he wants; and the woman who understands that she is raising royalty and that he is not meant to be a void-filler but rather the manifestation of everything she surrounds him with, and fills his mind, body, and spirit with.

I struggled with self-doubt and questioned how receptive single mothers would be to a young man offering to guide them through the difficult and often disheartening journey of boy raising. I wondered if mothers would be able to momentarily set aside any potential feelings and biases that would be evoked by hearing this message from a man. Adding to my uneasiness was the realization that this responsibility, which typically has been thrust upon millions of women, is not solely theirs to begin with. Nonetheless, many of you find the role your sole responsibility, whether right, deserved, planned or none of the above. I wrestled through my uneasiness and arrived at the conclusion that I was exactly who the mothers, aunts, cousins, grandmothers, godmothers, and foster mothers of the world—doing the seemingly impossible everyday—needed to hear from. It also occurred to me, from listening, observing, and reflecting on my own life experiences, that if parenting in general involves a degree of guesswork, raising a boy to become something that even the world's best mother will never be—a successful man—naturally involves *even more* guesswork.

Before I was even a teenager, I was the "man of the house" (in my mind). Many times, I stood amid domestic violence and helplessly absorbed, like a sponge tossed into a pool of water, the sight of a crying mother. I stood speechless toward a baby brother for whom I was too young, hurt, and dumbfounded to offer the right thing to say or do—whatever that might have been. At a young age, I came to grips with the realties of what it meant to go from two (already modest) blue-collar incomes to one. I watched how my mother bravely adjusted from working two to as many as five jobs simultaneously to keep things as "unchanged" as she could after the departure of my father left her to care for my brother and me. Now I sit here, a young man in my thirties, already having had experiences as a college athlete, a corporate professional, an attorney, a college professor, a mentor, a husband, a responsible father of two precious children, and 100 percent confident that I will change the world for the better in some way before I die (and therein will lie *my* "success").

Given the facts as they were leading up to my parents' separation and my mother taking the reins with two boys to raise on her own, it was not likely that my story would turn out as it has, and for millions, their similar story does not end well. However, the most important realization I have ever had was that my current position in life has as much to do with the circumstances and nature of my upbringing, both the positive and the negative, as it has to do with how hard I've worked to achieve my goals. The culmination of my experiences through high school, college, law school, corporate America, the criminal justice system, and the state child-welfare system has allowed me to objectively and unemotionally identify and analyze critical problems and issues with the way boys are being raised by single mothers. In vast numbers, our boys are not able to be independent, successful, thoughtful, productive, respectful, disciplined, intelligent, confident, well-adjusted, responsible, and self-aware members of society.

The days of my mother and grandmother—when raising a boy to a man was as simple as making sure he stayed out of trouble, graduated from high school, and respected his elders—are long gone. No matter how protective or vigilant a mother you might be, boys of today must be prepared to effectively navigate a world where racism, sexism, and classism are as much a part of their everyday lives as breathing. Beyond that, being uninformed or misinformed when it comes to sex, drugs, peer pressure, the value of self-worth and esteem, the criminal justice system, the value of education, financial literacy, the myth of entitlement, and the dangers of shortsightedness, will assuredly guarantee your son a long, miserable life, incarceration, or an untimely death.

You are not alone. The world has changed in so many ways, and no one has given our women a guide to accomplishing the most difficult thing they may ever do in their entire lives—raising a young boy to a successful, self-aware man without a father in the home. My thoughts will not help you raise a perfect man, as I am far from it. They will, however, give you many of the tools and perspectives you need to raise a great man. "Great" being a relative term, I foresee a day when single mothers will be raising men that are not only good in the eyes of the brave women who gave them life or raised them, but great in the eyes of humanity. It is then a possibility that this next generation of men—great men—will see to it to shift the paradigm back to strong, balanced family structures, unified in the purpose of raising amazing children.

I hope my book will alter your perspective, educate you, give you faith, revitalize your spirit, and encourage you to persevere. Where my words sound like criticism, it is out of love for my brothers; for the millions of women who have embraced, rather than abandoned us; and for my burning desire to see the day when society is more proud of its young men than they are afraid of and disappointed in them. No matter your race, nationality, or social class, women raising a boy without a strong, reliable, responsible, self-aware, man in the home share a common bond and a common challenge. You have within you the ability to change the landscape of society by dedicating yourself to the principles and ideas discussed in this book.

PART I
LOVING, SPOILING, AND CREATING THE ENTITLEMENT MONSTER

Special Delivery by Elijah Bourne

CHAPTER 1

ARE YOU CREATING A MONSTER?

Have you ever thought anything like the following?

- It's my fault that his father is not here, so I am going to be both his mother and his father.
- His father may not be here, but I will make sure he wants for nothing.
- We might not be rich, but I will make sure that none of his friends ever know.
- I never want my son to be embarrassed because he doesn't have something that everyone else has.
- He might only have one, but I am going to give him the love of two parents.
- I remember what it was like growing up without things—I never want my son to go through that.

If you have, then chances are that these thoughts are reflected in the way you are raising your son. What could possibly be wrong with thinking any of the above or raising a son with these thoughts in mind? What could possibly be wrong with wanting to make sure that your son does not go without simply because of your circumstances or your relationship with his father? On the surface, there is nothing wrong with any of these thoughts. However, for a single mom raising a son in today's world, these innocent and well-intentioned thoughts could be the beginnings of a monster in creation—by his very own mother. I like to refer to him as the "entitlement monster."

The entitlement monster does not understand why he cannot have what everyone else has, right now, or why you are telling him that he cannot (if you ever do tell him no). He does not understand—or believe—when you tell him that you cannot afford to buy something for him (if you ever do tell him that). He does not understand that you may be wearing old shoes so that he can wear new ones nor does he care. He does not notice that you may be wearing last season's fashions so that he won't be the only one without "it," whatever the "it" of the week happens to be. He doesn't understand, or care, that you have not gone on vacation in years because of the money you spend on his clothes, shoes, school tuition, housing, camps, and so on. If you are in the fortunate class of single mothers who has expendable income and a high-paying job, he doesn't understand that what luxuries you do afford him come at the sacrifice of other things. Similarly, he doesn't understand that even if you can afford to lavish him in whatever he wants, you don't *owe him* everything he wants—and neither does anyone else.

He doesn't understand why he should clean up after himself, wash his clothes when he is capable, mow the lawn, shovel the snow, or take out the trash. He doesn't understand why his goal should be to move out of his mother's home as soon as possible after graduating from high school or why he should contribute to household expenses if he does not move out. He does not feel guilty about spending every dime he makes on himself or his girlfriend as soon as he gets it and then asking you for money. He does not appreciate the sacrifices you have made and continue to make for him and will tell you in a heartbeat that you have never done anything for him, that he doesn't need you, or—even worse—that you don't love him. There are many other things that the entitlement monster doesn't understand nor does he care to understand.

So what does he understand? There is one thing that he thinks he understands—that he is entitled to what he wants, when he wants it. He understands that it is either your responsibility or society's responsibility to provide it for him—indefinitely and at his discretion. Furthermore, he understands that the things he wants in life should be his—not because he has worked for them, planned for them, or sacrificed for them but simply because he wants them. Anyone in his life, including you, who doesn't cosign this twisted and insanely backward perspective is regarded as *hostile* to him. "Hostile," in his eyes, means that you don't like him, you hate him, or you are standing in the way of what he wants for no good reason. There lies both the horror and the sadness of the myth of entitlement.

If you think that your sweet, innocent toddler or young boy who would move mountains for his mother could or would never become the person I've just described, you couldn't be more wrong. I'd venture to say that most entitlement monsters started off sweet as pie—and then something went terribly wrong. Despite the best intentions, many single mothers ingrain or foster the mentality and myth of entitlement in their sons either by things they actively do, things they neglect to do, or a combination of both.

Unfortunately, once a boy has bought into this myth, the damage is far more serious than the obvious undesirable effects on his personality. I call entitlement a myth because the idea that the world or the people in it owe you the desires of your heart and mind is a fallacy. The result is a teenager or young man who will not or cannot see how his actions and choices largely determine what he gets and does not get. He will not understand that what he has and does not have in life is directly impacted by his attitude and his perspective.

If his daily satisfaction in life has always been determined by the harmonious coexistence of two factors—what he wants and how his mother, or society, will ensure that he gets what he wants—then it is impossible for him to be happy when his mother is no longer ensuring that he always gets what he wants or thinks he needs. How can he be happy when society is not waiting to give him the things he wants? These things could be material, such as money, cars, jewelry, or clothes. They can also be intangible things, such as getting the job he wants, going to the school he wants, or being able to live where he wants to live. He will not be capable of valuing concepts like hard work and goal setting because in his life, goal setting and strong work ethic were either optional or not consistently *required* by his mother at all. Thus far, he has been entitled.

CHAPTER 2

THE DIFFERENCE BETWEEN LOVING AND SPOILING

FOR MANY MOTHERS, love for their sons is expressed in terms of what you do for them, what you give to them, and what you make available to them. These are pretty normal ways of expressing love. But these normal things you do for your son, such as making dinner, doing laundry, cleaning up after him, washing his dishes, driving him places, or always making sure he has money, can be misunderstood by your son as things you are merely supposed to do anyway.

He is right to some extent that much of what you do may be out of obligation to your child. However, the problem is not all these things that you do out of love, it is what you forget to do. It is these forgotten things that lead to a son being spoiled and his mother wondering how the hell that happened, behind her back and right under her nose.

What many single mothers forget to do is teach their son the value of reciprocating their love. A little boy is never too young to learn that love should be a two-way street. It is not necessarily something that he can be made to do, but something that he should want to do. At an early age, the reciprocation should be in the form of a simple thank-you. A young boy should not be comfortable taking or accepting anything from anyone (especially his mother) without thanking that person for it. If he is comfortable not saying "thank you" to people, it is because you have allowed him to be.

A little boy who does not say "thank you" will one day be a teenager who not only doesn't say "thank you" but also wants ten times more than he is willing to give. He will never engender the goodwill or favor that come from being thankful and letting those who give to him know that he acknowledges their generosity or kindness. Instill in your son as early as possible that people, including you, do for him and give things to him because they want to and choose to, not because they have to. Even though your love for him may be the driving force behind what you do for him, you are still choosing to do it, and that choice should not be taken for granted.

The reality is that if you teach your son to take you for granted, then he will. I really do not believe that any of us are born understanding the importance of being appreciative. Perhaps because we don't remember ever being literally taught this concept, we take for granted that we must consciously teach appreciation to our sons. There is truly a value in appreciating what is done for you, even if the "what" is something that is at its core intangible, like love. In fact, it is probably more difficult to appreciate something that cannot be touched or counted, so when your son learns to appreciate being loved and all the actions that stem from love, it will be easier for him to appreciate all of the tangible material items that one should also be thankful for. Once the basic concepts of appreciation are learned and become a part of who a boy is, it will be difficult for him to become spoiled. Being spoiled, unappreciative, and taking people for granted will feel uncomfortable, unnatural, and just plain wrong.

Once your son has learned the most basic ways to reciprocate love—that is, being thankful—it will be much easier to teach him the value of giving so that he may learn that people's time, effort, and eventually money are worth something. He will learn that whenever someone gives of any of these things for his benefit, he or she has made a sacrifice. This is impossible for him to learn, however, if you have never taught him as young boy the beauty of giving and the joy that comes (or should come) with that giving. More importantly, giving, in some way (there is no one right way) should be an integral part of his life.

Teach him that meaningful giving can have little and sometimes nothing to do with money. As a young child, there is a lot to be learned by making a get-well card, visiting a sick friend, or calling a grandmother just to see how she is feeling. There are valuable life lessons to be learned from baking cookies for a neighbor or helping mom make breakfast for the family.

I would venture to say that the best way to teach these concepts is primarily by modeling the behavior you want to foster in your son. I grew up seeing my mother constantly giving everyday, and I am pretty sure that she is responsible for the giving nature I have today. Living an appreciative, thoughtful, and giving life must be a way of life, not something that is done now and then. A child can tell the difference. He can sense your urgency, your sincerity, and your authenticity.

There is nothing wrong with explaining to your son why you do what you do and the reasons why you give. Do not underestimate what he will understand either. Children are notorious for understanding things that adults assume are too complicated for them, perhaps because as adults, we are often in the business of complicating simple things. What I am saying is actually quite simple: teach to thank and appreciate, teach to live a giving life, and model both consistently.

The spoiling comes in when mothers give and give and give, which is a natural part of mothering, but leave out the critical thank-give-model component of raising their sons. A spoiled boy will come to measure love in terms of what you and people in general can do for and give to him, while his role in the relationship will not even enter his mind. As he gets older, his needs and wants will become greater, his tastes more expensive, and his expectations of you higher by the day. If thus far you have been a bottomless pit of giving and sacrifice, neither expecting or demanding anything in return, how then can you consider changing the rules of the game ten, twelve, or fifteen years in? How can you no longer be willing to feed the ferocious appetite of the monster you have created? Hopefully you see how this chain of events could present a problem.

Mothers cannot be afraid to demand more than their sons voluntarily give. Chances are that whatever sons volunteer, if anything, is meaningless and merely a token representation of an ulterior motive—to stay out past curfew, to borrow money, or to use the car. If the boy is younger, the motives may be purer, but he still needs you as the older, wiser adult to set the bar to a higher standard than he will himself. It is never too early to ask yourself what you demand of your son in return for everything you give to and do for him. The reality is that you'd probably be doing those same things regardless of what he did or if he appreciated them or not, but that is not the point.

The first step is to take inventory of your relationship with your son and address the lopsidedness that will make itself obvious. And do not think that if you are middle class (whatever that is) or poor that you could not possibly be spoiling your son and that this could not apply to you. The reality is that for every wealthy, spoiled teenage boy, there is definitely a spoiled one whose mother works two or three jobs just to make ends meet. Get away from the mind-set that the entitlement problem I am talking about is a "rich kid" problem, because it is that errant thinking that has resulted in an entire generation of young men spoiled rotten, without the money to go along with the ailment.

CHAPTER 3

THE REAL WORLD AND RESPECTING THE THEORY OF CONSEQUENCE

Prisoner. College dropout. High school dropout. Felon. Drug addict. Juvenile delinquent. Underachiever. Weed head. Slacker. Deadbeat. Hoodlum. Thug. These are all labels that society places on many young men and teenaged boys. These labels are often misapplied and can reflect a callousness and ignorance to the multifaceted nature of what makes boys and young men who they are. However, some of the boys and men who are subject to this labeling often have something very similar in common. At the time in their lives when they needed it most, during the building of their personal foundations, they either were not taught, or did not buy into, the consequence theory of the "real world."

In the real world, there is a real and direct relationship between the choices one makes and the outcomes one experiences. The understanding of this relationship is one of the most powerful tools one can be armed with while navigating life. Without this understanding, most of our young men find themselves wandering, stumbling, and suffering through their lives. They wonder why bad things always happen to them, why the world is always against them, and why the odds are never in their favor. They are bewildered as to why doing things their way continues to yield the same negative, unsatisfactory, and painful results.

Understanding the consequence theory of the real world does not assume or presuppose for one second that there are not socioeconomic and other systems in place that impact and seek to negatively affect our lives. However, as a single mother raising a son, it is critical not to allow the existence of these systems to prevent you from arming your son with the understanding that he needs to successfully appreciate the power of thoughtful decision making.

Every child and young adult—every person, for that matter—makes choices and decisions that are unwise, risky, and often plain foolish. But as common people, it seems that we are separated into two groups when it comes to this human flaw of poor decision making. There are some for whom making poor, irrational, and thoughtless choices happens occasionally and infrequently, when they are driven to act impulsively or in the spur of the moment.

There are times when the most thoughtful person seems ruled and blinded, even if only for a moment, by pure emotion, whether it be passion, love, lust, greed, envy, excitement, or a variety of other gripping sentiments. For those in this category, there usually comes—shortly after they act—a feeling or intuition that maybe they've just made a poor decision. If not then, at least later, in the aftermath, as the dust settles and the consequences of whatever choice they made begin to manifest, they internally come to terms with the reality that the decision they made was a poor one. They long for the moment or moments they would gladly take back if only it were possible.

There are some in this group of people for whom the thoughts of wishing for a do-over sound too much like regret and reject that this notion is the end stage of self-checking or introspection. For these people, there is an acceptance of the reality that despite whatever other actors or factors may have been involved in producing the consequential outcome, they could have created a different, if not better, outcome by acting differently. People in this first group see the correlation between personal responsibility, choice, and consequences. They realize that something they did or did not do, or the way in which they did or did not do something, created a specific result. They "get it."

I'd venture to say that most young boys and young men are in the second group—those who do not "get it." Along the railroad track that is life, Poor Decision is not an occasional stop for this group of boys and men—they live, eat, sleep, and get their mail there. For them, poor decision making has become a way of life, and life has become a deep cavern too steep to climb out of, a road too foggy to navigate with any presence of clarity. This group totally underestimates, if they acknowledge it at all, the relationship between what they think, act, or do and the consequences that all of these bear.

As a result, they find themselves always asking the following questions:

- Why do I always get into trouble?
- Why did I get that grade?
- Why am I so unlucky?
- Why do these bad things always happen to me?

They are unable to realize that the answers to these and all similar questions often (*not always*, but often) relate directly to one or a series of poor decisions or choices they have made. Therefore, boys and young men in this group develop a false reality that can answer all of these questions for them without acknowledging personal responsibility and the consequence theory of the real world. Protected and comforted by this fake security blanket they've created to cope with the harsh reality of painful consequences, they navigate the world believing and telling anyone who will listen that they get bad grades because teachers don't like them. They don't get hired or lose jobs because the bosses didn't like them. Their mothers, family, and anyone else who care enough to offer an opinion are always on their backs because nothing they do will ever be good enough.

This second group of males, scores of whom are being raised by single mothers, need to be awakened, gently or harshly, to some realities that none of us are born knowing. The fact is that if you as a parent are in tune with these realities, you either learned it because someone taught you, or you learned it through observation and personal experience. Take a deliberate active stance in teaching your son, no matter how young, that he does have control of his destiny and that he does have control in determining his successes and failures. Show him how making one decision can lead to a good result, whereas making another can lead to a bad one.

CASE IN POINT

It's Friday night, and James has a science project due on Monday. He has started it but has not finished. You remind him that the project is due on Monday, and he says, "I know. I've got it covered, Mom." Sunday night comes, and the weekend has come and gone way faster than expected. James is exhausted and hands in a mediocre project. He explains to the teacher that he had a rough weekend and asks for an extra day to complete the project. The teacher says no. James passes but earns a very mediocre grade. He comes home to you and complains about how unfair his teacher is for not giving him an extra day to improve his project. The reality is that she could have given him the extra day. But what are the other realities? Do you side with James and berate the teacher for being unreasonable? Or do you have a conversation with James about how the different choices he made in the days and weeks leading up to the due date were responsible for his bad grade? Do you explain to him that the teacher did not OWE him an extension but that the extension would have been merely a *courtesy*? Do you say, "I told you so"?

Although many lessons can be learned through failure, they are not ones that can only be learned through negative life experiences. Seize the opportunity to teach your boy through his and other people's successes how the choices they made led to that success. A little boy who learns to write his name without help does so through practice, so seize that chance to teach him about the value of practicing as a way to learn and get better at anything. If you are a student or working mother and get a good grade or a positive review from your job, take that opportunity to teach your son how all those times he saw you reading, studying, or typing led to that good grade. Show him how all those hours you put in at work—with pride in what you were doing—led to your being recognized. When your son brings home a homework assignment with a sticker on it from his teacher, make sure he understands that he didn't get that sticker solely because his teacher likes him or because he's entitled to it but because he did something well to earn it. When he gets a compliment on how handsome he is, seize that opportunity to teach him the value of grooming himself and taking pride in his appearance.

Life is full of teaching opportunities and chances to instill in your son values and beliefs that will shape his perspective on life as a teenager and a young man. It is your responsibility as a parent to seize as many of these opportunities as possible and not to make the mistake of assuming that they will just "get it." As mothers and as a society, we cannot afford to continue taking that risk.

Moreover, once you commit to making sure your son can first recognize and then begin to understand the relationship between his actions and the way his life unfolds before him, you will see the effects of your commitment in his attitude, his perspective, and his actions. You might see it in his willingness to work harder, the pride he takes in his appearance, or the choices in the company he keeps. You will also see a child who is more likely to think about how his behavior may affect his life and the life of others around him.

As you commit to raising your son to understand that his actions have consequences, it is also important that he understand the possible limitations of the power he has to control his destiny. Consequences are real, but so are the attitudes and wills of other people who may chose to act a certain way regardless of what you do, what you say, how you carry yourself, or how hard you work.

Without regard to what you deserve, there will always be times when others attempt to give you less. The idea isn't to instill in your son that he can control every aspect and outcome of his life or what other people think or do. It is to guide him into a way of thinking that respects the theory of consequences, thus drastically affecting the chances of obtaining good or favorable outcomes if that is what he desires for his life.

CHAPTER 4

RUNNING FROM RESENTMENT INTO THE ARMS OF REGRET

AS SINGLE MOTHERS, sometimes it seems that you have to choose between being liked and being the mother you need to be for your son. Sometimes you find yourself in a position in which you know that denying your son what he wants or expects or not telling him what he wants to hear will cause him to resent you. I also understand that the common saying, "I don't care if you like me; I don't need you to like me" is easier to say when *thinking* about your tough-love approach toward child raising than it is to put it into practice in the heat of the moment, when all you might want is a little peace.

The fact of the matter is that sometimes being resented is a part of the parenting process. Being a single mother means that there are times when you have to burden the resentment share of two parents, because for whatever reason, Dad isn't there to shoulder his part. It is a well-accepted fact that regardless of what people may say, everyone desires to be liked, and the relationship parents have with their children is no exception to that desire. However, the temporary resentment that a single mother has to face is more than worth the consequences of raising a boy who will be abused and knocked down by life at every turn because he is unarmed and unprepared to process what life is throwing at him. The challenges he will face won't wait until he graduates from high school either. The challenges of life don't care when your son turns eighteen or when he graduates from high school, for they will come at him in one form or another as soon as he begins socially interacting with the world.

Take resentment head on rather than running from it. There will be times, if you try hard enough and are patient enough, when you can converse and reason your way right through the angry wall of resentment. But I have learned that taking a son head on can mean many different things to different mothers.

I have seen some mothers take on a very aggressive, confrontational stance when dealing with their sons, often because they believe that this stance is a necessary one that a man would take with him. I have learned that many mothers believe that by being hard, aggressive, and confrontational with their sons, they are "toughening them up" or "teaching them to be a man." However, what I have observed is that sometimes a mother's nurturing role is completely replaced by a perceived need to be a disciplinarian *all the time*. No mother should have to completely forsake her role as a lover and nurturer. Likewise, no mother—especially a single mother—should completely forsake her role as a disciplinarian. Every mother, especially single mothers, should be constantly seeking to find the balance between the two and resisting the perceived need to be 100 percent one way or the other. The result of either extreme will have drastically negative effects on your son and your relationship with him.

In between parenting out of fear of resentment and not caring at all about creating resentment is an elusive but existing middle ground. Finding the balance sometimes seems impossible, but persevere, and seek wise counsel from *successful* mothers and *great* men. When you are successful, you will see that you may have averted future resentment and made promising and valuable gains in the real-world education of your son. Over time, these gains will culminate to result in your son staying out of prison, getting through high school or college, and avoiding becoming a father prematurely. He'll have the foundation to make him a responsible, successful, thoughtful member of society.

PART II
ARE YOU DESTROYING YOUR SON'S SELF-WORTH?

Mom's Love

Miracles happen when a child is born
Outstanding, amazing love is turned on
Mother and child can take on the world
Someday the big picture will finally unfurl
Love is an adventure to a hidden place, and
Over the course of time things find their place
Varieties of challenges are waiting for you but
Everyone must try their best to pull through.

- Chloe Bourne
© 2016

CHAPTER 1

WHICH SIDE ARE YOU ON?

Have you ever noticed or heard of any of the following behavior in boys:

- Not participating in class
- Not willing to try out for sports teams even though they love the sport
- Intentionally not working to their potential in school
- Surrounding themselves with other boys who aren't about anything positive
- Turning to gangs or potentially deviant social groups for acceptance
- Suffering from depression

Have you ever noticed any of the following behaviors in young men?

- Little or no feelings about hurting others
- Low or no sense of value for human life
- Inability to maintain a relationship with a woman who has goals or is otherwise focused on making progress

- Tendency to indulge in addictive behaviors like smoking and alcohol abuse
- Tendency to be violent toward women
- Tendency to overcompensate by being flashy and excessive in their obsession with material things

As you may recall from being a teenager, much of our youth is spent finding and defining, whether consciously or not, who we are and where we fit in. From the youngest age we can remember, our social identity has a definite impact on our self-identity. Arguably, the relationship is actually the other way around, and it is our own self-perception that eventually defines or determines our social identity. Either way, for most of us, there is a constant struggle of self-definition that challenges our ability to adapt to our changing selves, the changing of the people around us, and their attitudes.

This constant self-evolution continues from childhood through puberty to young adulthood and even into adulthood. Rarely, however, does anyone explain to us that how we define and identify ourselves can either be our catapult into a happy and fulfilled future or the shackles that bind us to negativity, dissatisfaction, and the fear of fulfilling our destinies. Even more rarely, does someone sit us down and say the following:

"You are great."
"You are precious."

"You are valuable simply because you ARE."
"You are valuable simply because you are here."
"Your worth is immeasurable."
"Your life has a purpose."
"Your purpose is to accomplish great things."
"The world will be a better place because of your life."

What I am talking about is instilling the value of self-worth, which will create self-esteem for your son. I do not believe you can have high self-esteem without high self-worth, and for too long, too many have failed to make the connection between the plight of young boys and men and their lack of self-worth and self-esteem. Somewhere along the way, self-esteem became mislabeled as a young girl or woman's issue, a problem that starts affecting many women when they are young girls. If not addressed, it follows them into adulthood, creating havoc in their personal and private lives alike. What society and single mothers raising boys have to understand as soon as possible is that lack of self-esteem is not a female issue, and the effects on our sons have been and continue to be devastating.

CASES IN POINT
Charles and Joe
Charles is thirteen years old. He is a freshman in high school and loves to play basketball. Unfortunately, he is

rail thin at 130 pounds, and shorter than everyone who was on the team last year. He has never played organized basketball for a team but does well when he plays in recreational pickup games at the park, which he's done for years. Despite all of these challenges, Charles thinks to himself that he might have a shot, although a slim one, of making the freshman team if he tries out for it. But then again, the others are bigger, surely faster, and have an air of confidence and arrogance—they *know* they are the best. Charles can picture making a complete fool of himself as he tries out for the team—falling, getting stripped, missing lay-ups, and so on. He decides not to try out for the team this year. In the years to follow, he becomes less and less interested in playing basketball at all and tells himself that he really didn't like it that much in the first place.

Joe is in the same exact position under the same exact circumstances. He knows he's good, but he's not sure if he's as good as they other guys trying out. He tells himself that he's going to give it his best shot and that the worst thing that can happen is him not making it this year, in which case maybe he'll try out next year. Joe tries out and, though he is probably too small, impresses the coaches with his agility and his positive attitude. He makes the team. He becomes better and bigger every year until his senior year. He is now seventeen years old, has gained forty pounds, and is five inches taller. He is offered a basketball scholarship to a local university.

- What is it that made Charles not try out for the team?
- Would it surprise you to know that Charles was actually a better basketball player than Joe?
- What is it that made it harder and harder for Charles to decide to try out in the years after his freshman year?
- In what ways did that decision Charles made when he was thirteen possibly affect the course of his life?

Quincy and Terrell

Quincy is a nine-year-old in the fourth grade. He gets average grades and is well known for his tendency to be the loudest one in the room. He often gives teachers the impression that he is not really paying attention, but when called on, he engages in discussion with the teacher far above the level of his peers. Despite his behavior issues and, quite frankly, a lack of manners and respect for authority, an English teacher sees potential in him and his ability as a thoughtful young speaker. The teacher suggests to him that he join the debate team. She even sends a note home to his mother encouraging the idea.

Quincy is caught off guard and nervous at even the thought of standing in front of people and talking. "Am I even good enough to be on a debate team?" he thinks. "Man, my friends will laugh at me. Nobody cool is on the debate team anyway." Quincy decides he's not joining the debate team, and by the way, his mother never gets that note from the teacher either. He ends up getting expelled for mouthing off to teachers on repeated occasions. He has to repeat the grade because he is too far behind to catch up.

Terrell is in the same exact predicament. He has average grades, poor self-control, lack of discipline, and a tendency to annoy even the most patient teacher to no end. But he definitely has a gift for understanding issues and talking about them on a level that exceeds his fellow nine-year-olds. The same English teacher suggests the debate team to Terrell and gives him a note to take to his mother. Terrell doesn't know if he'll like the debate team but never doubts that he is capable of doing it. Part of Terrell feels like he can do anything well "if he really feels like it." None of his friends are on the debate team, and, almost certainly, they'll laugh him into next week when they hear about it. "So what if they do?" thinks Terrell. "There must be a reason she asked me and not them." Terrell gives the note to his mother and asks her what she thinks. She is doubtful about whether he is capable and how it will affect him if he is not. Nevertheless, she encourages her son to give it a try.

Terrell joins the debate team and excels. He eventually becomes captain, and the team is featured throughout the local news. He goes on to the debate teams in high school and college and eventually becomes a successful attorney.

- What was it that made Terrell give the note to his mother despite his questions?
- What was it in Terrell that made him not make the decision based on what his friends would say?
- What do you think doing well, becoming the captain, and getting featured in the local news did for Terrell's confidence?
- Can an experience at the age of nine really have an impact on the direction of a kid's life?

Having a firm sense of self-worth doesn't mean that you think you are God's gift to the world (though we all are in my opinion, I'm referring to the expression as it is used to convey a disdainful arrogance) or that you have no fear of failure. It certainly doesn't mean that you do not care at all what other people think about you. What it does mean is that you realize that without trying, you will never know for sure what you can do or what you are made of. Without trying, you are depriving yourself of what you deserve and what you are worth—the opportunity to do something good. When you realize your self-worth, you are in tune with the reality that you are worth more than your potential failures and that those failures do not make you any less valuable, because you are already valuable. You are in tune with the fact that you are worth the effort of striving to achieve a goal.

There is a direct connection between what you think of yourself and your tolerance for mediocrity, which makes you hide from the challenges of life. The lower your self-worth, the higher your tolerance for underachievement and the more likely you are to hide, like Charles and Quincy, from anything that might call your false sense of security into question. The higher your self-worth, the higher your tolerance is for risking failure but not necessarily for failure itself. Like Charles, it is important for boys to realize that fear is natural and normal but that fear cannot be where their decision ends or what their decision is based on. Charles realized that a chance at making the team was more valuable than the security of trying and not doing as well as everyone else. Unlike Charles and Quincy, Joe and Terrell didn't hide from the challenges, because whether they realized it or not, something in them knew that they were worth the effort of trying and the risk of failing. They were worth the chance to be great.

All children, like adults, want to be accepted to some extent. It is critical, however, to realize the difference between the normal social need or desire for acceptance and being totally consumed and defined by what other people think. A boy with low or no self-worth is going to be so consumed with being liked and accepted that he will do anything to be "cool."

The difference between the boy who will deprive himself of a great opportunity out of fear of seeming "uncool" or not "down" and the boy who will take that opportunity, despite having fears or doubts, is self-worth and self-esteem. Unfortunately, this difference manifests itself in a variety of sad and depressing ways—namely, poor decision making and chronic underachievement, which usually leads to joblessness, homelessness, or incarceration.

More than ever before, tune your antennas to your son's self-worth and self-esteem frequencies. When you see him shying away from challenges, avoiding great opportunities, and otherwise being ruled by fear—step up and step in. Talk to him. Talk him through his thoughts about why he is avoiding whatever it is he is avoiding. Do not accept "Because," "I just don't feel like it," or "No reason" as answers. There is always a reason. There is a reason for everything.

CHAPTER 2

HIDING IS A HABIT, BUT SO IS ACHIEVING

When issues of self-worth and self-esteem in a boy are not addressed, they do not merely go away. The issues lead to a behavior that reflects who he has become. Most likely, it is someone who does not think very highly of himself, is very afraid to fail, is overly conscious of what people might say and think about him, and, most telling, lives his life in a way that allows him to avoid challenge and discomfort as much and as often as possible.

What is more troubling, though, is that the repetitive nature of avoidance becomes second nature so that he might not even know he is doing it, and as his parent, you may not be involved enough in his life to know that it is going on. Frankly put, hiding is a habit. And just like any habit, especially bad ones, it is very hard to break. Like Charles in the basketball example above, not trying to make the team his freshman year set the tone for how he'd approach making the team every year thereafter because it got increasingly difficult for him to face the challenge. Now imagine a young man who has been in the habit of hiding since he was a little boy—in kindergarten, elementary school, junior high school, high school, and beyond. How difficult is it going to be for him to realize that he is still in hiding, let alone to break the hiding habit?

What's also telling about the habit of hiding is that boys who are alike in this way will flock together and surround themselves with like-minded people. They generally will not align themselves with people who are knocking down doors and living challenging lives—these people are reminders of what they are not. So to a large extent, what I grew up hearing my mother say about "birds of a feather" is true.

There are many variations of the hiding habit. One of the more common varieties is that of the serial quitter. The serial quitter is often uncomfortable with the outside pressure (like a parent constantly questioning them) that comes from avoiding every potential challenge of life. Sometimes he is genuinely interested in something. Either way, he will dive into a challenge head on with a refreshing sense of enthusiasm. The problem begins, however, when he is not immediately successful at the new endeavor or when immediate success doesn't last long. The serial quitter, who actually has low self-esteem, is then faced with what he perceives as two potential outcomes. He can work harder and dedicate even more time to becoming better at what he is doing, after which he might still fail. Or, he can quit now and save himself the effort, time, and disappointment of putting his all into something and still failing at it. Lacking the confidence to persevere, the sense of self-worth to take the chance, and the vision to be incentivized by long-term goals, the quitter quits.

In another variation, your son realizes the obvious implications of quitting and the likely disappointment he'll face from himself and others who care about him. He is not comfortable with the label "quitter." So what does he do? Does he go all out and give it his all just to prove a point? No, he doesn't. Instead he puts minimal or half of an effort into everything he does.

This behavior, in his mind, will guarantee that no one can ever call him a quitter. If people think he's truly trying, they'll just leave him alone and not pressure him to try harder or do better. This thought process applies to his schoolwork, sports, chores, and other parts of his life. In his mind, if he is trying, then he can't be criticized—he is safe from scrutiny and judgment. The sad part about this lifestyle is that this strategy of not fully applying himself or not putting his heart and soul into anything he does often achieves the effect he is looking for. He convinces people around him that he is doing the best he can do. They come to accept his underachievement and mediocrity as normal, and their expectations of him sink lower and lower as the years go by because they have come to believe that he is doing his best. Now they become complicit—accomplices and enablers in his cycle of mediocrity.

By the time many boys are in their late teens, they have no idea what it is like to put their absolute everything into something. The expression "blood, sweat, and tears" means nothing to them. The concept of sacrificing time, body, and mental capacity for a team is completely foreign. The experience of sacrificing immediate pleasures for grueling practice in another area that will pay off in the long term is not one they're familiar with. They don't know how it feels to give everything they have and fail but then regroup, learn from their trial, and carry on. They don't know how it feels to give everything they have and achieve the very thing they sacrificed and worked extremely hard for.

Are these young men, never having had these experiences, ready to face the harsh realities of the real world? Are they prepared to compete against other young men who have years, even decades, of experience putting their all into every single thing they do? Absolutely not. All they are prepared to do is continue down the road of mediocrity and disappointment in an increasingly competitive, typically unkind, and unforgiving world.

As a single mother, it is important to recognize in your son the behaviors associated with hiding as early as possible and to redirect him from this self-deprecating pattern. Don't make it so easy for him to quit. Many parents are comfortable with the fact that "he just doesn't like it anymore." Sometimes that may be true, but take the time to get to the bottom of the quitting. You may find that the obstacle causing him to quit is something with a simple solution. If you never try to get to the bottom of it, you will never know. And if your son is never given the opportunity to explore and articulate his feelings about why he wants to quit something, he may never come to realize the true rationale motivating his actions.

I remember as a child excelling through the Cub Scouts at record speed, absorbing new information, and piling up badges and awards faster than anyone else around me. And then I quit. To get to the next level, I had to pass a swimming test, and I had no idea how to swim. As ridiculous as the thought was, I had convinced my elementary-school mind that learning to swim just wasn't something I would ever be able to do.

I don't recall ever sharing this with my mother or my father, who was in the home at that time. But I don't recall them ever really asking either. I have absolutely no doubt in my mind, given all of the things I have achieved since then and the type of person I became through my adolescent years, that I could've been an Eagle Scout. This is the highest recognizable rank in the Boy Scouts of America and a very difficult one to reach. But I took myself out of the game. I am truly thankful that after that, I made *achieving*—not *quitting*—a habit.

What's also important is trying to instill in your son how important it is to put his all into everything he does, even when the task is not necessarily his favorite. Don't be so quick to assume that he is already doing his best.

Just as adults often seek advice from others when we already know the solution to our problem, boys need for you to ensure that they are doing what they already know they should be doing. He might be a C student, but with some investigation on your part and some fine-tuning, he could really be a B or an A student. He might be an OK swimmer, but maybe with some extra attention to his weaknesses, he can be a great swimmer.

If you truly believe that your son has innate gifts and that it is only a matter of exposing them, then you will be genuinely motivated not to accept mediocrity and under-achievement. This motivation on your part will result in your son becoming a more confident and successful young man.

Like hiding and quitting, however, achieving is also a habit. When a boy gets used to doing good things, whether for himself or for other people, it will become second nature. Likewise, when a boy has many opportunities to go through the process of self-doubt, fear, acceptance of a challenge, and achieving a successful result, he will come to expect success. Achievement will not be a surprise to him, especially when he has worked hard toward it. With each success comes a boost in self-worth and thus self-esteem, and the confidence from one achievement will surely spill over to all other areas of his life.

Again, the point is not for your son to get to a state of complete fearlessness but rather to be confident enough to believe that he is worth the effort, pain, and sacrifice that achieving worthwhile goals typically requires. The point is for your son to believe that he is worth the effort and worth the risk of failing if the potential result is a worthy reward for himself or someone he cares about. The habit of achieving leads directly back to your responsibility as a parent because it should begin with you.

CHAPTER 3

CREATING OPPORTUNITIES FOR GREATNESS

Whether they tell you or not, boys are looking to their parents—and if you are a single mother, to you primarily—for reassurance. They are looking for reassurance that they are valuable, loved, accepted, special, and capable of achieving great things. As the parent, the primary responsibility for creating these "opportunities for greatness," as I like to call them, does not lie with the school, the city, or society—it lies with you.

CASE IN POINT
Marcus and Darren

Marcus's mother is satisfied with the progress fifteen-year-old Marcus is making in school, but she is concerned that she is losing touch with him and that he is totally self-absorbed. Even worse, he takes everything he has and everything she does for him for granted. She talks, fusses, and yells at him, trying to get him to understand that he is spoiled and will not always have her to spoon-feed him. Frustrated with him and his nonchalant attitude, she decides to let things take their natural course, as there seems to be no way of getting through to him.

Marcus ends up spending less and less time at home and eventually affiliates with a gang. He barely finishes high school and continues down a path of selfish, self-destructive behavior.

Darren's mother is going through the same thing, and she worries that her son has no regard for anyone but himself and his circle of friends. He wants for nothing yet can quickly come up with a list of all the things he wants but does not have. Darren's mother decides that she is going to teach her son a lesson in humility and service, or at least she is going to try. Against his will, she gets him to change his "busy" schedule. One Saturday morning, takes him to a soup kitchen nearby, where they volunteer serving food to the homeless, washing dishes, and cleaning up the kitchen.

It's not as much of a "waste of time" as Darren thought it was going to be, and his mother convinces him to bring a friend with him the next time. His mother can no longer go with him, because she has to work, but Darren continues to go on his own. He develops a good relationship with the staff at the shelter and even some of the people who come in for food and assistance. Realizing that there is a level of need in the community that he had never really paid attention to, he decides that when he finishes his education, he wants to be a community activist. Darren starts to feel a great sense of purpose, accomplishment, and joy in what he is doing and the big difference his hour or two each week makes in the lives of so many people. Darren's mother begins to see an all-around change in him—for the better.

- Is Darren's selfish attitude and unrealistic perspective of life common in teenagers?
- Marcus's mother and Darren's mother were both "good parents," but what was the difference between them?
- Can you think of other ways by which these two mothers could have taught their sons a lesson in humility and service?
- What do humility and service have to do with self-worth and self-esteem?

The story of Marcus and Darren plays out every day across the world. So many of our young boys are consumed with fear—of failure, of rejection, of being laughed at, of stepping outside of the box—that they are literally crippled by their self-defeating attitude. In the face of this, doing nothing is not an option for single mothers. Unless your son has had opportunities to be great, he will not know how to seize them when they present themselves. *He may not even recognize them* when they present themselves, and if he can "hide" from those opportunities instead of taking them head on, he will.

How do you create these opportunities? Where are they? They are everywhere. In the schools, there are athletic teams through which he will have the opportunity to learn the lifelong lessons of teamwork, responsibility, accountability, hard work, and perseverance, even if he is not the star of the team. They are in the Cub Scouts and the Boy Scouts, where they will learn the values of creativity, bravery, respect for nature, and survival. They are in the church, where there are opportunities to participate in youth groups, choirs and bands, and many leadership forums. They are in the schools, where there is a club with elected officers for almost every interest under the sun. They are in the community organizations like the Boys and Girls Club, the United Way, the YMCA and the Police Athletic League, in which opportunities to build self-esteem and interact with positive adults and youth abound. And the opportunities are in the countless people in and surrounding our communities that could benefit from the spirit of volunteerism, such as senior citizens, the homeless, and sick and shut-in people.

Of course, with any activity or organization outside of your home, it is critically important to do your homework on the organization and its leaders so that you know personally who will be influencing and supervising your son. There is no substitute for your own thorough investigation, face-to-face interaction, and your intuition. All institutions and all leaders are not created equal, and unfortunately, everyone who claims to have good intentions does not. However, the opportunities are out there to be seized, and your son will benefit greatly from them if you seek them out, do your homework, and choose wisely.

Your son might not be an athletic all-star, but there is just as much pride to be taken in being an all-star at helping the less fortunate, playing a musical instrument, acting, singing, writing, painting, dancing, or mastering computer technology. Though money is definitely a reality that may limit the activities your child can participate in, there are many opportunities for youth to do great things that will strengthen their sense of self-worth and increase their self-esteem that don't cost a thing but time and energy, on their part and yours. Just as we consider money in the stock market an investment, so is time well spent putting your son in a position to learn, grow, and win. Just as we consider our personal relationships an investment of our time and resources, so is time sacrificed to open otherwise closed doors to your son's future. Decide to make the investment.

CHAPTER 4

THE MEASURE OF WORTH: ARE YOU SENDING A CLEAR MESSAGE?

JUST AS LIFE is challenging your sons to be extraordinary when it is so convenient to be ordinary, life is also challenging you, the single mother, to prioritize and continuously reassess your role as a parent. Before you resolve yourself to the notion that you can't afford these opportunities for greatness, ask yourself where you may have spent an extra few hundred dollars last year. It has always amazed me how a struggling parent could spend hundreds (even thousands) of dollars on Christmas gifts or athletic shoes, yet resolve herself to defeat when faced with an SAT-preparation course fee. Though costly, it can make the difference between college admission and rejection, scholarship or impossible tuition payments. If you are in a position in which you can choose, your son's future cannot afford for you to choose the fantasy holiday, the ridiculously expensive athletic shoes, or the designer jeans over the tutoring, the SAT class, the registration fee for sports camp, or the uniform fee for Cub Scouts.

Besides, your son will be able to tell, based on your actions, what your priorities are and what you want his priorities to be. If you constantly preach to him about how important it is to do well in school but do nothing to change or address the situation when he doesn't do well, what message are you sending? If you tell him that you can't afford the karate lessons or the piano lessons or the registration fee for summer camp but spend the money elsewhere on things that are clearly not necessities, then what message are you sending?

Without even realizing it, sometimes mothers shut their sons out of opportunities that they do not see as realistic. This is simply because they have a misconception that such a goal is unattainable and that certain opportunities are inaccessible, when in fact that is not true. The opportunities are there if you look—you owe it to your son to find them and seize them.

Capitalize on any spark of talent and ability you see in your son, and nurture that spark. The only difference between some of the most famous people we've ever heard of and the many more we have never heard of is often the nurturing of that spark of talent. If your son takes to the water like a fish, take him down to the YMCA for lessons or to join the swim team. If you little boy runs like the wind, sign him up for the community track club. If your little boy loves to draw, find an art class to enroll him in. If he loves to ask questions and loves to talk, get him on the debate team. If he is too young for certain activities at school, take the lead yourself. You'd be amazed at how our personal interactions with our sons can shape the way they think, relate, argue, articulate, and reason. When you constantly find yourself looking for the spark, and trying to figure out how to nurture and grow it, then you are realizing the value of your son's self-worth and on your way to ensuring that he will have a healthy sense of self-esteem.

Don't be afraid to be proactive either. As a modern-day parent, you are fighting a battle against materialism and shallowness like no generation of parents has ever had to fight before. In an environment where it is so easy for children to feel like they are less valuable people if they do not have certain material things or are not wearing a certain brand of clothes, the parent has to consciously and deliberately fight that poisoning and destructive mentality. Surprisingly, instead of fighting that mentality, many parents foster and support it. Often, it is more important to the parent that their "little man" get his Jordans than it is to the child, who could often care less what he wears as long as it doesn't look bad!

The point is not that there is anything inherently wrong with nice or expensive things. The point is that a child's sense of self-worth and value should not be connected to the label on his shoes or shirt. Instill in your son the value of taking pride in his appearance, regardless of what he is wearing. Instill in him the value of cleanliness and refinement. Instill in him the self-confidence to, at some point, be able to develop his own tasteful sense of style and class.

What is the point of wearing really expensive clothes or jewelry if the clothes do not fit or do not complement your body? We've all seen it. What is the point of flashing all of the designer labels if your hygiene is not in order? We've all seen it. What is the point of looking like a million dollars on the outside if you are empty, weak, and discontent on the inside? We've all seen it…and maybe even been there ourselves.

The truth is that a boy who sees his own self-worth tied to material possessions will see the people around him the same way. And so it becomes a little easier to use people (including you), to sell drugs for money to buy the latest thing, or to steal from someone. Because in his mind, people are not inherently valuable—they are valuable only for and because of the things they have.

Many facets of our society are certainly doing their job when it comes to indoctrinating our children. Good mothers raising sons have to consistently remind themselves how important it is to do their jobs as well.

PART III
RAISING A GOAL-ORIENTED SON BEGINS WITH YOU (NOT YOUR SON)

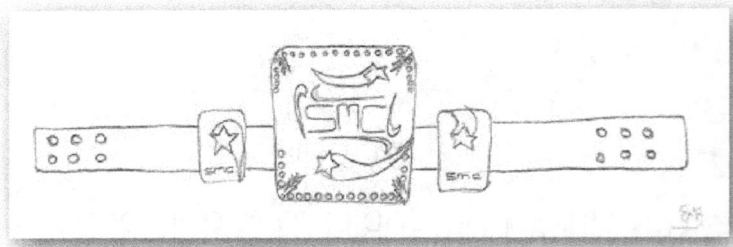

The Single Mom Championship by Elijah Bourne

CHAPTER 1

SEEING, THINKING, AND LIVING BEYOND TODAY

"Take one day at a time."
"Worry about today; tomorrow will take care of itself."
"Live every day like it's your last."

THESE ARE SAYINGS that we've all heard in life at one time or another. Some of us may even live by those words and directly or indirectly encourage our sons to live by them too. Each of these sayings has its own measure of wisdom. But when taken out of context or applied to our lives in the wrong way, these same sayings can be representative of an ideology that continues to slowly destroy generations of our sons. They can be, despite the infinite wisdom within them, the foundation of a perilous way of thought and life.

Raising the goal-oriented son begins with you. Specifically, it is initially based on your expectations of your son, not on your son's inherent desires or self-motivation. If you expect little or nothing of your son, then your parenting will reflect your expectations or the lack thereof. Likewise, if you do not acknowledge that goal setting is an integral key to any degree of accomplishment or success in life, no matter how old you are, your parenting will reflect that belief. Just as harmful, many of us are conditioned to think of conscious goal setting either as a strictly adult exercise or as an exercise that only some have the luxury of performing. Neither thought could be further from the truth.

In reality, it is very difficult and unrealistic for an adult to start living life by setting goals if he or she has not lived life that way for the past two decades. The practice of continually challenging yourself to project a future success or achievement is an audacious and, at times, downright scary one. The accountability that accompanies goal setting, even if it is only to oneself, often causes most not to set goals at all or, possibly just as bad, to set them beneath one's potential.

There is usually a direct relationship between goal setting and fear or feelings of inadequacy. We see this relationship play itself out in our everyday lives and the lives of those around us. Many places in this world, there is a boy who runs faster than anyone around him but won't try out for the track team. Many places in this world, there are fathers who are miserably stuck in a dead-end job but refuse to pursue the career of their dreams. Do you know the young man who "took a break" from college to collect himself only to find reason after reason every semester why he "can't" go back yet? Do you know the young man who has convinced himself that average grades are acceptable even though he has above-average potential? They all have some issues in common—all related to the fears associated with goal setting. But their actions of procrastination, hopelessness, quitting, and underachieving are just the outward manifestations of their internal attitudes regarding goal setting.

They either have forgotten or have never been taught and nurtured to live in a constant cycle of goal setting—that is, setting, working, failure or success, self-analysis, and adjustment. Living in a cycle that involves the boldness and vulnerability of goal setting, and possibly failure, is learned. If you are a single mother raising a boy, you must teach this behavior. Is it possible that your son might pick it up from someplace or someone else? Possibly, but unlikely.

CHAPTER 2

BUILDING A FOUNDATION FOR A GOAL-SETTING SON

I AM CERTAINLY not the first to recognize that goal setting is not merely an adult exercise. All you have to do is read the latest advice on potty training and tooth brushing to realize that even small children recognize and appreciate the relationship between their actions and rewards. Despite this knowledge, parents often forget that a boy's expectations and goals for himself matter just as much, if not more, than the parent's expectations of him.

For example, having children become independent is a tremendous goal—for parents. As we are often exhausted and stretched to the limit, we yearn for the day when they are potty trained, brushing their teeth on their own, dressing themselves, sleeping in their own beds, and cleaning up after themselves. For many of us, our sons may grow up and start shaving before all of these desires are fulfilled! But in the midst of our goal setting, it is easy to forget that these accomplishments can, and should be, the child's accomplishments as well. Besides, if you have encouraged your son to want these things for himself and put a time frame on them (no matter how loose or far out), then you have just given him his foundation for living a life that encompasses goal setting.

Undoubtedly, there will be failures. There will be accidents. However, your son can learn that these accidents and failures are good even though they may make him feel bad. As parents, it is up to us to teach our young children that making mistakes and sometimes failing is a valuable part of learning, growing, and succeeding. The value is in finding out where we went wrong or where the mistake was made and what should be done differently the next time around to get the success we want. So your son got pee on the toilet seat—next time, he should lift the seat up first and not wait until he is about to explode before going to the bathroom. So your son dripped toothpaste onto his shirt—next time, he should lean over the sink more. So your son drenched his sleeves while he was washing his hands—next time, he should slide his sleeves up before washing his hands. The list goes on and on.

Sometimes being a busy parent, especially a single parent, causes us to miss the real accomplishments—the triumph within the triumph—when it comes to our children. The real victory is not that you no longer have to buy diapers or that your child is not soiling himself several times a day anymore. The real triumph is that child's realization that he can consciously decide to do something by himself and successfully. The superficial triumph is in succeeding. The real triumph is in the cycle—or the process—of success: trying, failing, doing differently, trying again, and then succeeding.

Of course, depending on the circumstances we grew up in and what our parents' philosophies on child raising were, understanding the value of, let alone teaching a child about, living the goal-oriented life is easier said than done. Many parents abhorred mistakes and responded by yelling, demeaning, or even beating their children when relatively meaningless mistakes were made. Others may have had a lot of autonomy, growing up in a hands-off type of environment in which there wasn't a lot of scolding, but not a lot of coaching and reassuring through mistakes either. No matter where your experience falls in this spectrum, making decisions that will foster a goal-oriented way of thinking for your child is in his best interests and yours.

Remember the following:

- The child that is too afraid to make mistakes will be too afraid to set goals.
- The concept of learning from mistakes is learned. Our body may have an instinct to avoid harm (like not touching a hot stove twice), but the self-analysis that allows us to step back, assess, regroup, and try again in a different manner is learned and becomes more instinctive the more it is done.
- Your child needs to know that you have his back—and love him and believe in him just the same—despite his mistakes.

REWARDING GOAL SETTING AND ACCOMPLISHMENT BUT TEACHING THROUGH FAILURES AND SHORTFALLS

If there is one thing that children understand, it is the reward system. Do not be afraid to set one up for your children. It may come as a surprise to you that the best rewards are things that you either already give your child or will give them in the future, for no reason at all other than because they ask for it or because you want them to have it. For example, things like candy, toys, and snacks are excellent motivators for young children—especially if they can't have them whenever they want to. For older children, it may not be as easy, but it is easy to forget that certain things they may consider rights are actually privileges—for example, watching television, going to the movies or shopping, getting an allowance, and borrowing the car. The days when things like fast food, going to the movies, and being taken shopping were considered "treats" or otherwise "special" have gone away. Parents are responsible for that change in culture, many would say, to the detriment of our children.

CREATING GOAL CHARTS

I'm a believer in the theory that a thought is more meaningful and more powerful once it is written. Practically speaking, a goal chart is a great way to introduce the concept of goal setting to young children. Simply set out a list of goals and designate a time frame for them. If your child is old enough, have him participate in setting the goals. Examples of the most primary goals are dressing and undressing, putting away toys, brushing teeth, and using the potty consistently. For the older child, the goal chart could include completing daily chores and earning good grades at school. For the teenager, who definitely should be participating in the creation of his own goals, the chart could include various academic accomplishments like achieving a certain test score, extracurricular achievements like athletic goals, financial goals like saving a certain amount of money by a particular time, or life achievements like getting into particular colleges or earning scholarships.

As your son gets older, you realize that what your goals are for your son become less and less meaningful—it is what your son's goals are for himself that will make him either a success or an underachiever. The foundation, however, comes from you. After building this foundation, you will see how goal setting transcends home life and filters into every part of your son's life such as school, work, sports, and extracurricular activities. In my opinion, the following are examples of things that do not happen unless they are goals set by the child:

- getting college scholarships
- making the honor roll
- saving enough money to independently buy what he wants

- achieving in athletics
- learning foreign languages

When you teach your son how to become a goal setter, he will do it instinctively—naturally. The point is not to be so driven by goals that he loses the ability to live freely. The point, however, is to be self-driven, with a direction and a point of focus. From a reflective perspective, think back on your life:

- What have you achieved that you are really proud of—by accident?
- What difficult journey have you completed without first setting out to do it?
- Have you ever talked yourself into doing something you knew wouldn't be easy and then succeeded at it? Remember how good you felt?

MISTAKES AND CONVERSATIONS

The last thing you want is a son who is so afraid of disappointing you that he sells himself short on his dreams and aspirations—even if they are merely those of a child. There are some detrimental mistakes, despite good intentions, that are often made by mothers raising boys. Some of them are discussed below—ask yourself if any of them sound familiar to you.

CHAPTER 3

THE SHORT SELL

Do not let your own fears about not getting it right when it comes to raising your son cause you to sell yourself short as a parent. For any parent, there will be some degree of learning on the job when it comes to parenting for you too. You will not get it right every time, and you shouldn't expect yourself too. Assuming that you are acting in your son's best interest and not your own, when you make decisions concerning him, worrying never helps at all. Throughout his life, you will have to make important decisions such as what school to send him to, whether or not to let him play a sport, and who his friends should be. You will never have a crystal ball to help you make these important decisions.

Second-guessing yourself and adding more stress to what is already a stressful decision making process never helped anyone. By example, you can teach your son that when mistakes are made, the best thing to do is acknowledge, evaluate, regroup, and move on, intent on not repeating the mistake.

Do you discourage your son from setting high goals and standards because you don't believe he is capable of reaching them? Not all of us are fortunate enough to have come from parents or families with long track records of outstanding achievement, success, or stability. Because of that, many single mothers, some knowingly and some unknowingly, lower the bar for their sons when it comes to achieving anything that really matters.

Sometimes, a lifetime void of personal relationships with successful men, whether it is a father or any other relative, can lead a mother to assume that mediocrity or failure is their son's destiny. The painful truth is that only you can really search your soul to assess your genuine expectations for your son. Only you can really evaluate yourself and determine whether or not you believe in the potential for greatness that lies within your son.

If you do not believe it, your doubt will be transparent, no matter how hard you might try to hide it. Depending on your son's personality, your doubt might inspire him to prove you wrong. Maybe your doubt will fuel your son to be one of the most memorable entertainers, athletes, academics, or politicians of his time. More than likely, however, it will merely plant a seed of self-doubt and inadequacy in him that will fester and grow in him until it manifests itself in every aspect of his childhood and adult life, causing him to never be great at anything that really matters.

Kids do not always live up to the expectations of their parents, but rest assured, the children of parents who have no expectations of them (or low expectations of them) have little to live up to. For a single mother raising a son, this concept is even truer. Despite your income, despite your circumstances, despite single parenthood, *expect greatness from your son.* Make it clear as early as possible that he is destined to reach the stars and that his potential is limitless. Never let him forget that the only true impediment to his success is and will always be him. Most importantly, let him know that you believe in him. Every son needs, wants, and craves this assurance from his mother.

PROTECTING YOUR SON FROM THE PAIN OF POTENTIAL FAILURE

A mother's natural instinct is to protect her child from hurt and pain, including that of failure. This is understandable. However, without the counterbalancing of a parent who recognizes that failure can be an extraordinary tool for growth and success, sons are usually done a great disservice by their well-intentioned mothers.

You will be hard-pressed to find anyone in history that has accomplished great feats accidentally, without a goal, and without ever failing. In fact, most great feats, no matter what area of life, are preceded by painful failures. Consider the following examples:

- Michael Jordan was cut from his high school basketball team before going on to become arguably the greatest basketball player in the history of the game.
- President Barak Obama lost (badly) a Democratic primary election for the US House of Representatives before going on to win subsequent elections and eventually, the United States presidency.
- Many of the world's most successful entrepreneurs such as Bill Gates (Microsoft), Sir Richard Branson (the Virgin Empire), the late Steve Jobs (Apple), and Mark Zuckerberg (Facebook)—the list could go on forever—all experienced

devastating professional or academic failures and setbacks before going on to become some of the most successful, wealthy, and famous people in the world.

The key is how your son, first as a boy and later a man, learns to deal with the hurt and pain that often comes with failure and setbacks. History has proven that adversity builds champions, stars, and world changers. Yet mothers, especially single mothers, would shield their sons from any and all adversity if given the chance. Though this urge may be instinctive, it is damaging to your son and will continue to handicap him well into adulthood. Even worse, you will have created in your son an inability to deal with disappointment, adversity, and failure and killed any desire he would have had to take chances and face his fears. When faced with the choice of thinking big and setting lofty goals, he will be inclined to take the easy way out and avoid the risk of failing if that is what he has learned from you.

In a practical sense, this means that when your son comes home wanting to quit something he has barely started because things got tough, it is *your* responsibility to talk him through his emotions and not let him quit. When your son decides not to pursue something you know he loves or enjoys, it is *your* responsibility to talk him through his fears and make him realize that he should not eliminate himself from "the game." When your son comes to you with a bright idea that seems destined to fail, it is *your* responsibility to be a voice of encouragement, guidance, and wisdom, not the voice of negativity and defeat.

The hardest pill to swallow may very well be that in your attempts to protect your son from any and all discomforts associated with failure, what you are actually doing is creating a man who will be an emotional cripple, handicapped by his own fear and stuck within the four corners of self-imposed mediocrity. On a larger scale, you could also be depriving the world of the next Barack Obama, Dick Gregory, Muhammad Ali, Russell Simmons, Jim Brown, or Mark Zuckerberg.

CHAPTER 4

THE GOAL-SETTING BOY BECOMES THE GOAL-SETTING MAN

THERE ARE MANY realities in life that some of us never accept, or worse, never become aware of. Among them is the reality that there is a direct link between setting goals and becoming successful at anything. Some of us embrace this reality as mature adults, but a minority of people—a fortunate segment of society—learn and embrace this reality as teenagers and even as young children. Your son can and should be one of these children. Your son needs you to teach him to be one of these children.

We often don't think about it in these terms, but very short-term goals dictate much of what we do on a daily basis. On days when you are tired and don't feel like going, you go to the grocery store to buy food anyway because that would affect your goal of not starving. You may not want to get up and go to work on a particular day, but you go because that could affect your goal of staying employed. You don't buy new clothes every time you see something you like because that would affect your goal of saving for something more important like vacation or Christmas presents or paying the rent. When thought of in these terms, it becomes more and more apparent how critical it is to set and stick to short-term goals. Now imagine how your life and the lives of those around you would fall apart if you didn't set any short-term goals or if you only tried to accomplish them every now and then instead of consistently. You'd be homeless, without food, and living on the edge of existence.

Imagine all of the things you'd like your son to accomplish as a child or teenager—academic honors, athletic achievements, playing an instrument, or getting or finding a great job. (If you do not aspire for your son to find and achieve his purpose, start giving this thought. You are a vital part of this process.) Is it logical to expect someone who is not a goal setter to accomplish any of these things? The unfortunate reality is that it is not logical or realistic to expect someone who hasn't set goals to achieve goals. If left unaddressed, a child will become a teenager and then an adult who is unprepared and incapable of accomplishing anything substantial in life if he is never taught the value of setting and working to accomplish his goals.

For your son, long-term goals are just as important as short-term goals. Doing things like maintaining quality relationships, getting into and finishing college, getting valuable summer internships, and developing lifelong skills require long-term goal setting.

It is our goals, whether short-term or long-term, that guide us toward sensible decisions and away from erratic, thoughtless ones. It is goals that stop a boy from repeatedly impregnating girls. It is goals that stop a boy from shooting someone after an argument. It is goals that stop a boy from cutting school. It is goals that stop a boy from binge drinking and then driving. It is goals that stop a boy from becoming a drug dealer. A boy who has no worthy goals in life lives like he has nothing to lose. He lives like the decisions he makes today will have no effect on his future. He lives like he is not in control of his future. He lives like his life is happening to him and not like he has the ability to make his life happen.

CHAPTER 5

HIGH SCHOOL, COLLEGE, AND THE REAL WORLD

ONE OF MY best friends once told me that college is merely representative of the fact that a person can start something and finish it. It is a four- or five-year-long endeavor that says one is capable of setting a long-term goal and achieving a succession of often-difficult short-term goals on the way to achieving it. There is a lot of truth to this theory.

College is also representative of another important life reality that is far more important than the degree that is earned—it is not enough to want something. There is something between wanting it and getting it. Far too often, our sons are deluded into believing that they should have things simply because they want them. It is as if there is no requirement to do the part in the middle—or as if there is no part in the middle. So what typically happens when a boy or young man gets a dose of reality? He either quits, abandoning his goal, or does something really illogical in attempt to get it, such as breaking the law.

People often refer to life after college as "the real world." I remember someone asking me after I graduated: "How does it feel to be in the real world now?" I remember being a bit insulted, although I knew the person didn't mean to be insulting. But I knew that the past four years of my life had been very difficult and that I had worked very hard to earn the grades I was given while also doing a lot of other things for my university and my community.

The sacrifices I made and the relationships I developed during those four years were the "part in the middle" between my high school diploma and my acceptance to law school. They were also responsible for my first job in corporate America. When adults refer to high school and college as time periods that are not "the real world" they perpetuate a misperception about the urgency and importance of those periods in a boy's life. Sure, some people have the luxury of being mediocre or goofing off until they figure things out. For some, no matter how much they underachieve, they will still eventually always end up in position to be successful if they so chose. However, adults foster an ill perception of college (and even high school to some extent) as unlike the real world, and thus the sense of urgency is not there.

Every year, thousands of students fail out of college after their first semester or first year because of the overwhelming difference in freedom between high school and college. "You mean to tell me that if I don't feel like getting out of bed, nobody is going to make me?" or "You mean to tell me that if I don't show up in class, the professor is not going to call my house to tell on me?" True indeed. Nobody is coming to pull you out of bed, and nobody's calling home to your mother to tell on you. But you will be put out of school, and that tuition will be due—and that is very much how the real world works.

I've spoken to a lot of high school and college students about the value of internships, especially summer internships. I've told mentees repeatedly that they should not let a summer go by in which they are not building relationships, obtaining new skills, and adding a valuable new experience to their resume. Those who take heed typically end up with amazing experiences that not only make them more marketable but also enhance their lives. But still some do not and end up working a menial summer job or doing nothing at all because all of the best opportunities are already taken. That reality is very much reflective of the real world.

Our teenagers and young adults, in college and out, will have to navigate the world of acquaintances, friends, and enemies. Deciphering who is who and distinguishing how to move among them is very much a real-world experience that does not wait until later in adulthood to confront our teenagers and young adults.

Still, for many reasons, we either consciously shield our sons or subconsciously neglect to prepare them for these realities of the real world. Perhaps there is a sense of denial about how soon in life these themes will be relevant to them. Perhaps there is a denial about how soon in life they will need the skills to navigate these seemingly very adult predicaments.

Regardless of the reasons, the reality is that not knowing how to deal with these realities in a mature way will serve as obstacles to your son's goals. Your job as a mother goes far beyond nurturing (feeding, clothing, and loving). It also includes preparing them for the realities of life and preparing them to be capable of achieving goals if they set their hearts and minds to them. The latter is typically the missing piece of the puzzle.

CHAPTER 6

WANTING IT AND GETTING IT: THE GREAT DIVIDE

IMAGINE STANDING ON the edge of a bridge overlooking the river that lies beneath and separates you from the land on the other side. The land across the river isn't so far away that you cannot see it, because the river isn't that wide, but it is there, nonetheless. In fact, you can even see that there are people on the other side, so you know that it is possible to cross, though you don't know exactly how they got there. In a crucial moment of decisiveness, you decide that you want to be there. Now what?

For some boys, goal setting is not the problem—the imagination and willingness to dream and set goals overflows with ease and abundance. Then reality sets in, and the thrill fades away as the great divide becomes more and more apparent. Goal setting alone is not enough. There is something that matters between wanting it and getting it.

When your son was an infant, you provided everything he wanted without a second thought. He wanted milk; you immediately gave him milk. He wanted food; you immediately gave him food. He wanted a toy; you immediately gave him the toy. He was cold; you immediately swaddled him in a blanket. As he gets older, this will inevitably continue—his needs and wants will be expressed and immediately met by you, often without question.

How you get what you are giving to him is seldom, if ever, a consideration for him. How you earn the money and what you sacrifice to get him what he wants doesn't matter to him. To a certain extent, it shouldn't matter, depending on how young he is. But where does his luxury of being completely oblivious to the reality of your sacrifices end? At what point do you inform him that there is something that has to be done—work, effort, planning—to get him the things that he wants?

Teach your son that there is something between wanting and getting. Teach him that once he decides he wants something, he should not just expect it to appear and to be handed to him. Teach him the thought process necessary to identify how it is he is going to get what he wants. Is he going to work for it? Save up money for it? Study for it? Research to learn how others have obtained what he wants? Teach him to create and execute a plan—even if he needs assistance from someone else in executing.

The mind-set that "I want, and therefore it should be given to me now by any means necessary" is a dangerous and unrealistic one. Yet it is one that plagues most of society's boys and men today. Millions of boys and men have been incarcerated or killed because they never learned, or refused to adhere to, the concept of planning and working to achieve a goal legally. Putting your son in a position in which he understands this thought process—bridging the gap between what he wants and his goal—is your responsibility.

PART IV
THE NECESSITY AND POWER OF MENTORING: WHERE DO I BEGIN?

Original art by Michael Tudor, Jr.

CHAPTER 1

THE VALUE OF MENTORING

WHETHER WE WERE conscious of it or not, at some point in time, someone or some combination of people showed us how to be the men and women that we are. It may have been a parent, an aunt or uncle, or the parent of a friend who you spent a lot of time around. It could have been people in the neighborhood who were adults, or peers who were only slightly older than you.

For better or for worse, we took pieces of character, personality, and perspective from these people and made it our own. In today's society, these people are often formally called mentors. As a child, your son will want to dress, act, talk, and be like someone or some combination of people who he looks to as models. The problem is that these models do not necessarily have to be positive ones and often are not. It is, however, human nature to look outside of ourselves for answers and guidance.

As mothers raising boys, especially without a father in the home, it is very important to expose your sons to people who can play a mentoring role. As a mother, your perspective and approach will likely embody a mothering, nurturing, feminine perspective. With that said, simply teaching what society associates with masculinity—for example, aggressiveness, strength, and callousness—does not and could never replace positive, intelligent male mentoring. Contrary to popular belief, manhood is not the opposite of womanhood. And to be sure, it is certainly a nebulous concept with nuances that are morphed by time, culture shifts, and geography. Moreover, manhood is not exactly the same to each and every man. Exposing your son to a variety of positive male influences will provide him with different perspectives and examples of manhood that will hopefully have, at their core, the same code and value system.

There are certain things about manhood that have to be learned, either by overt teaching or by simply absorbing lessons, or "jewels," through exposure. Your son may never be explicitly told, "A real man works, supports himself, and supports his family," but he may see the role a mentor plays in his household. Your son may never be told, "A real man is dependable, and his word is everything," but he may see that in the way his mentor handles his business. Your son may never be told, "Never handle domestic disputes with violence," but he may have a conversation with a mentor who shares a personal anecdote that teaches that very sentiment. Your son may never be told, "A man is judged by the company he keeps," but he may observe the thoroughness of his mentor's people and take note. Your son may never be told, "True manhood requires that you respect yourself and those around you at all times," but he may understand this reality after being educated by a mentor regarding society's misleading messages about the meaning of respect and how it is earned.

Although any mother could literally talk to her son about these aspects of manhood and have him repeat them verbatim, that teaching, while valuable, can never replace the influence of mentoring by a responsible male figure or male community. Why not? Mentorship can never be replaced by mothering because your son wants to learn from and be valued by something he can see himself becoming. If your son is a boy, what he inevitably sees himself becoming is a teenaged boy, then a man. This is why the allure of "the streets" is so attractive to boys. The younger boys are strongly influenced by teenaged boys, and teenaged boys are strongly influenced by the adult men. We are always looking to the visual images of what we hope to become or think we will become, whether we want to or not. Despite how nurturing, strong, beautiful, or intelligent of a mother you might be, your son simply cannot look to you as a future version of himself. Additionally, even though you might say all of the right things, your message will always be questioned because it is coming from someone who will never actually be what he will be, yearns to be, and hopes to be—a teenaged boy and then a grown man.

CHAPTER 2

WHERE AND HOW TO FIND MENTORS

The word "mentor" is very common in some circles. In others, it is a word and concept that many have heard before but is still surrounded by some mystery. An often-asked question (and frankly, a logical one) is "Where can I find a mentor?" Well, there is no one place to look. A good mentor can be found in a wide variety of places. Here are some examples:

YOUR OWN FAMILY

While there are some families who do not have within them one single positive male figure worthy of the title of mentor, there are probably just as many families who have untapped positive males with mentor potential within them. Ask yourself a few questions. Are there males in your family who meet any of the following criteria?

- are entrepreneurs
- own or have owned a business
- have gone to college

- have learned a trade and are using it to support a family (barber, plumber, electrician, pharmacist, home improvement contractor, landscaper, computer technician)
- have worked in a profession that is of interest to your son
- have traveled to foreign countries and might be willing to share their world view
- have a reputation for being hardworking, dedicated, and honorable

If this sounds like any of the males in your family, you may very well have someone who is mentor material.

YOUR PLACE OF WORSHIP

Good men and good mentors can often be found at places of worship. They are often in positions of leadership and knowledgeable about the challenges associated with the stages of manhood. Most of the time they will be career oriented, educated, and committed to continually becoming better men. However, as we all know, none of the above is necessarily the case. As with any potential mentor, you should take the time to get to know him and build a relationship with him so that you can judge whether or not he would be a positive influence on your son's life.

YOUR COMMUNITY

Potential mentors in our very own communities are often overlooked even though we interact with them regularly. The following professionals are typically easy to find in our communities:

- doctors
- nurses
- bankers
- prosecutors
- defense attorneys
- judges
- dentists
- optometrists
- counselors
- teachers
- principals
- police officers
- firefighters
- coaches
- martial arts instructors
- chefs and restaurateurs
- mayors
- city councilmen and councilwomen
- business owners and entrepreneurs

How would you go about getting access to these people for your son? There are several different ways you could make that happen. For one, you might already know them—for example, your son's dentist or teachers. You might be surprised at the welcoming response you get when you ask, "Would you mind talking to my son about what it took for you to become a _____?" or "My son loves to _____; would you mind sharing with him what your experience as a _____ is like?" or "My son is in the _____ grade and would love to know what a day in the life of a _____ is like — is there any way he could shadow you for a few hours one day?"

What is your son interested in? What does he enjoy doing? What are his strengths or talents? Introducing him to potential mentors and fostering those relationships will change your son's life.

CHAPTER 3

MENTORING AND DEFINING MANHOOD

SOME MAY DISAGREE, but there are certain characteristics that are wonderful to possess for everyone, regardless of gender. However, for each of these characteristics, how they are demonstrated and called upon in everyday life can be affected by gender for a whole host of reasons. How a man is called upon to demonstrate trustworthiness, loyalty, courtesy, kindness, obedience, positivity, bravery, reverence, humility, perseverance, leadership, and responsibility may at times be different that the ways women are called upon to display many of the same characteristics and attributes. And when it comes to fatherhood, even the best mother in the world will have her limitations regarding how to build, teach, and sustain manhood in a male child.

A male mentor can be extremely valuable to your son, especially when it comes to helping him find his way through a path to manhood that is typically a winding one with many bumps and roadblocks along the way. When a boy lacks a proper foundation and guidance from positive male figures that he identifies with in some way, he will create and exhibit his own ideas of what he believes being a man is. When a boy lacks masculine energy to balance the feminine energy he is receiving from his mother, he has a deficit that he will seek to fill in some way, shape, or form, whether positive or negative.

Without a decent foundation and without positive and diverse male mentorship, these self-created ideas typically manifest themselves in negative and often self-destructive ways. For example, if a boy believes that manhood is measured by how many women he can obtain, collect, or demand the attention of, this belief will shape his goals, desires, and actions. Inevitably, he will attempt to prove that he has succeeded at being a man by obtaining the ultimate proof or embodiment of his warped perception of manhood—children. It won't matter nearly as much with whom as it will how many.

The desire to recklessly reproduce children without thought regarding the practical realities of their futures stems from a warped perception of manhood. At a much deeper level, this perception likely stems from conscious or subconscious feelings of inadequacy and lack of self-esteem. Both of these, however, can usually be traced back to a disconnect from his father or father figure, or from not being raised by a father at all.

The right mentors will teach your son that producing children has nothing to do with being a man, because every man is born with the ability to procreate with a woman. The right mentor will teach your son that impregnating a female is not an accomplishment but that the true accomplishment is raising a son into a man that changes the world for the better. The right mentor will teach your son that his manhood is reflected in the decisions he makes regarding when to have children and who to have children with. The right mentor will teach your son that a man who does not feed, support, and nurture his child is not a good father and is instead a disgrace and a poor representation of a man.

A boy might also erroneously believe that manhood is measured or proven by aggression; the more aggressive he is, the manlier he is. This aggression manifests itself in many ways—a short temper, violence, and hostility, to name a few. His ability to differentiate when it is appropriate to be aggressive from when it is not will be distorted because this ability is taught and learned. Furthermore, if your son is in an environment where not being overly aggressive is perceived as being weak, he may learn to "turn up" or act even more aggressively than necessary as a defense mechanism or a survival mechanism.

The right mentor will teach your son that manhood is reflected in having the judgment to decide when aggression is necessary, or unnecessary, to achieve a desired result. The right mentor will teach your son that a man who cannot control his temper and whose actions are determined by his fleeting emotions is foolish and is actually weak. The right mentor will teach your son that manhood is reflected by his ability to consider the consequences of his actions before he takes them, not after.

Another example, and perhaps the most common misperception when it comes to manhood, is that manhood is defined by virtue of possessing money. While there is great value in both financial stability and the ability to support one's family, there is little value in merely possessing money if the man who possesses it is a fool. In other words, manhood is reflected not only in how one obtains his money but also what he does with it when he gets it.

Growing up without a father, or without one who provides and actually raises his son, typically contributes to financial instability. Exposure to the effects of financial hardship and deprivation, without the proper guidance and education, often feeds the misperception that possessing money is life's ultimate goal and the sole key to happiness.

The right mentor will teach your son that while many will not question where his money comes from or what he had to do to obtain it, how he obtains it matters. At what cost he obtains it matters. What he has to risk to obtain the money matters. The right mentor will teach your son that once he has the money in his possession, what he does with it matters.

The right mentor will teach your son the value of saving, investing, and budgeting his money so that he is not desperately starting over from scratch with nothing of value to show for it soon thereafter. The right mentor will teach your son the difference between appreciating and depreciating assets and the value of being able to leverage credit.

You might not be confident about the value of mentorship, and you might even doubt that anyone would care enough about your son to be his mentor. I guarantee you that you are wrong. And I guarantee you that your son is worth the effort. Your son, your community, and the lives of everyone your son will touch are depending on you. Be brave enough to be the best mother you can possibly be for your son.

EPILOGUE

DARE

Daring and daunting is the task
No better yet, chore – no – responsibility – or blessing?
You undertook, with understanding, or maybe none at all
Of what it would take, and require, and drain, and give
To your life
Again and again, what difference could it make, how hard could it be?
From what you were, what you came to be, a girl, and a woman
Oh what a surprise, how different they are
How strange they can be, so full of fire and dangerous curiosity
Either way, you are mom, with father or without
In a predicament of the ages
What do I make him? What will he become? For what purpose will he serve?
To love or to be loved? To hold or be held? To serve or to be served? To care or to be cared for? To provide, or to be provided for? To protect, or to be protected? To lead, or to be led? To discipline or be disciplined?

And if so, for how long?
When do you let go? When do you transition? Mother forever? Friend always or never? Mentor and guide or passenger along for the ride?
So many questions….Dare to ask
The right people, the right ones…

-MABJR
©2016

www.ingramcontent.com/pod-product-compliance
Lightning Source LLC
LaVergne TN
LVHW051505070426
835507LV00022B/2939